Easy Home Cooking ™

ALL NEW
SLOW COOKER

Publications International, Ltd.

Front cover photography by Sanders Studios, Inc.

Pictured on the front cover: Chicken Stew with Dumplings *(page 38)*.

Pictured on the back cover: Chicken Fajita with Cowpoke Barbecue Sauce *(page 50)*.

ISBN: 0-7853-3330-4

Manufactured in U.S.A.

8 7 6 5 4 3 2 1

The publisher would like to thank the following companies for the use of their recipes in this publication: Butterball® Turkey Company; Perdue Farms Incorporated; The Rival Company.

Contents

Welcome to Slow Cookers

Slow cookers can prepare almost any type of food you can imagine: hearty soups and stews, creative chicken, pork and beef recipes, and exciting party fare. Inviting the family over for a relaxed Sunday afternoon meal? Surprise them with *French-Style Pork Stew (page 31)*. Have a case of the blues? Comforting *Chicken Stew with Dumplings (page 38)* is just the thing to make you smile. By following the easy recipes in this magazine, you can prepare wonderful meals without a lot of fuss.

Slow cookers were introduced in the 1970's, found new popularity in the 1990's and are guaranteed to continue their growth into the new millennium. Considering the hectic pace of today's lifestyle, it's no wonder so many people have rediscovered this time-saving kitchen helper. Spend a few minutes preparing the ingredients, turn on the slow cooker and relax. Low heat and long cooking times take the stress out of meal preparation.

THE BASICS

• Slow cooker recipe time ranges are provided to account for variables such as temperature of ingredients before cooking and how full the slow cooker is during cooking. Once you become familiar with your slow cooker you'll have a good idea which end of the range to use.

• No peeking! A slow cooker can take as long as twenty minutes to regain the heat lost when the cover is removed. If the recipe calls for stirring, replace the lid quickly.

TIPS AND TECHNIQUES

Adapting Recipes: If you'd like to adapt your own favorite recipe to a slow cooker, you'll need to follow a few guidelines. First, try to find a similar recipe in this publication or your manufacturer's guide. Note the cooking time, liquid and quantity and size of meat and vegetable pieces. Because the slow cooker retains moisture, you will want to reduce the amount of liquid, often by as much as half. Add dairy products towards the end of the cooking time so they do not curdle.

Selecting the Right Meat: A good tip to keep in mind while shopping is that you can, and in fact should, use tougher, inexpensive cuts of meat. Keep top-quality cuts for roasting, broiling or grilling. You will be amazed to find even the toughest cuts come out fork-tender and flavorful in a slow cooker.

Reducing Fat: The slow cooker can help you make lower-fat meals because you won't be cooking in fat as you do when you stir-fry and sauté. Many recipes call for trimming excess fat from meat; be sure to do so. If you do use fatty cuts, consider browning them first on the range-top.

Chicken skin is high in fat, so most recipes call for skinless chicken. Also, chicken skin tends to shrivel and curl in the slow cooker. If you use skin-on pieces, brown them before adding them to the slow cooker.

Food Safety Tips: If you do any advance preparation, such as trimming meat or cutting vegetables, make sure you then cover and refrigerate the food until you're ready to start cooking. Store uncooked meats and vegetables separately. If you are preparing meat, poultry or fish, remember to wash your utensils and hands before touching other foods.

Once your dish is cooked, don't keep it in the slow cooker too long. Foods need to be kept cooler than 40°F or hotter than 140°F to avoid the growth of harmful bacteria. Do not reheat leftovers in the slow cooker! Use a microwave oven, range or oven for reheating.

By following these simple techniques and using the marvelous recipes in this publication, you will soon be preparing wonderful dishes with minimal effort.

In the Beginning

Chicken Wings in Honey Sauce (page 10)

Chicken Wings in Honey Sauce

3 pounds chicken wings (16 wings)
 Salt and black pepper to taste
2 cups honey
1 cup soy sauce
½ cup ketchup
¼ cup oil
2 cloves garlic, minced
 Sesame seeds (optional)

SLOW COOKER DIRECTIONS

Rinse chicken and pat dry with paper towels. Cut off and discard wing tips. Cut each wing at joint to make two sections. Sprinkle wings with salt and pepper. Place wings on broiler pan. Broil 4 to 5 inches from heat 20 minutes, 10 minutes a side or until chicken is brown. Transfer chicken to CROCK-POT® Slow Cooker.

For sauce, combine honey, soy sauce, ketchup, oil and garlic in bowl. Pour over chicken wings. Cover and cook on Low 4 to 5 hours or on High 2 to 2½ hours. Garnish with sesame seeds, if desired.

Makes about 32 appetizers

Hot Mulled Cider

½ gallon apple cider
½ cup packed light brown sugar
1½ teaspoons balsamic or cider vinegar
1 teaspoon vanilla
1 cinnamon stick
6 whole cloves
½ cup applejack or bourbon (optional)

Combine all ingredients in slow cooker. Cover and cook on LOW 5 to 6 hours. Discard cinnamon stick and cloves. Serve in hot mugs.

Makes 16 servings

Party Mix

3 cups bite-sized rice cereal
2 cups O-shaped oat cereal
2 cups bite-sized shredded wheat cereal
1 cup peanuts, pecans or cashews
1 cup thin pretzel sticks (optional)
½ cup butter or margarine, melted
4 tablespoons Worcestershire sauce
Dash hot pepper sauce
½ teaspoon seasoned salt
½ teaspoon garlic salt
½ teaspoon onion salt

SLOW COOKER DIRECTIONS
Combine cereals, nuts and pretzels in CROCK-POT® Slow Cooker. Mix melted butter with remaining ingredients in small bowl; pour over cereal mixture in CROCK-POT® Slow Cooker and toss lightly to coat. *Do not cover CROCK-POT® Slow Cooker.* Cook on High 2 hours, stirring well every 30 minutes; turn to Low for 2 to 6 hours. Store in airtight container.   *Makes 10 cups mix*

Spiced Apple Tea

3 bags cinnamon herbal tea
3 cups boiling water
2 cups unsweetened apple juice
6 whole cloves
1 cinnamon stick

Place tea bags in slow cooker. Pour boiling water over tea bags; cover and let stand 10 minutes. Remove and discard tea bags. Add apple juice, cloves and cinnamon stick to slow cooker. Cover and cook on LOW 2 to 3 hours. Remove and discard cloves and cinnamon stick. Serve in warm mugs.

Makes 4 servings

Viennese Coffee

3 cups strong freshly brewed hot coffee
3 tablespoons chocolate syrup
1 teaspoon sugar
⅓ cup heavy cream
¼ cup crème de cacao or Irish cream (optional)
  Whipped cream
  Chocolate shavings for garnish

Combine coffee, chocolate syrup and sugar in slow cooker. Cover and cook on LOW 2 to 2½ hours. Stir in heavy cream and crème de cacao, if using. Cover and cook 30 minutes or until heated through.

Ladle coffee into coffee cups; top with whipped cream and chocolate shavings.

Makes about 4 servings

Easiest Three-Cheese Fondue

1 tablespoon margarine
¼ cup finely chopped onion
2 cloves garlic, minced
1 tablespoon all-purpose flour
¾ cup reduced-fat (2%) milk
2 cups (8 ounces) shredded mild or sharp Cheddar cheese
1 package (3 ounces) cream cheese, cut into cubes
½ cup (2 ounces) crumbled blue cheese
⅛ teaspoon ground red pepper
4 to 6 drops hot pepper sauce
Assorted fresh vegetables or breadsticks for dipping

Combine all ingredients *except* fresh vegetables in slow cooker. Cover and cook on LOW 2 to 2½ hours, stirring once or twice, until cheese is melted and smooth. Increase heat to HIGH and cook 1 to 1½ hours or until heated through. Serve with fresh vegetables or breadsticks.
Makes 8 (3-tablespoon) servings

Hint: For a special touch, sprinkle fondue with parsley and ground red pepper.

Lighten Up: To reduce the total fat, replace the Cheddar cheese and cream cheese with reduced-fat Cheddar and cream cheeses.

Turkey Meatballs in Cranberry-Barbecue Sauce

1 can (16 ounces) jellied cranberry sauce
½ cup barbecue sauce
1 egg white
1 pound ground turkey
1 green onion with top, sliced
2 teaspoons grated orange peel
1 teaspoon reduced-sodium soy sauce
¼ teaspoon black pepper
⅛ teaspoon ground red pepper (optional)

Combine cranberry sauce and barbecue sauce in slow cooker. Cover and cook on HIGH 20 to 30 minutes or until cranberry sauce is melted and mixture is hot, stirring every 10 minutes.

Meanwhile, place egg white in medium bowl; beat lightly. Add turkey, green onion, orange peel, soy sauce, black pepper and ground red pepper, if desired; mix well with hands until well blended. Shape into 24 balls.

Spray large nonstick skillet with nonstick cooking spray. Add meatballs to skillet; cook over medium heat 8 to 10 minutes or until meatballs are no longer pink in center, carefully turning occasionally to brown evenly. Add to heated sauce in slow cooker; stir gently to coat evenly with sauce.

Reduce heat to LOW. Cover and cook 3 hours. When ready to serve, transfer meatballs to serving plate; garnish, if desired. Serve with decorative picks.

Makes 12 servings

Turkey Meatballs in
Cranberry-Barbecue Sauce

Steaming Chilis

Southwest Bean Chili (page 20)

Southwest Bean Chili

1 can (15 ounces) garbanzo beans, rinsed and drained
1 can (15 ounces) red kidney beans, rinsed and drained
1 can (15 ounces) black beans, rinsed and drained
1 cup chicken broth
4 cloves garlic, minced
1½ cups frozen corn
2 medium green bell peppers, seeded and chopped
1 can (16 ounces) tomato sauce
1 can (14½ ounces) Mexican-style stewed tomatoes, undrained
3 tablespoons chili powder
1 tablespoon cocoa powder
1 teaspoon ground cumin
½ teaspoon salt
   Hot cooked rice
   Shredded cheese, ripe olives, avocado and green onion slices
   (optional)

Combine all ingredients *except* rice and toppings in slow cooker. Cover and cook on LOW 6 to 6½ hours or until vegetables are tender.

Spoon rice into bowls; top with chili. Serve with shredded cheese, ripe olives, avocado and green onion slices, if desired.

Makes 8 to 10 servings

Chili Verde

¾ pound boneless lean pork, cut into 1-inch cubes
1 large onion, halved and thinly sliced
6 cloves garlic, chopped or sliced
1 pound fresh tomatillos, coarsely chopped
1 can (about 14 ounces) chicken broth
1 can (4 ounces) diced mild green chilies
1 teaspoon ground cumin
1 can (15 ounces) Great Northern beans, rinsed and drained
½ cup lightly packed fresh cilantro, chopped
   Sour cream

Spray large skillet with nonstick cooking spray and heat over medium-high heat. Add pork; cook until browned on all sides.

Combine cooked pork and all remaining ingredients *except* cilantro and sour cream in slow cooker. Cover and cook on HIGH 3 to 4 hours. Season to taste with salt and pepper. Gently press meat against side of slow cooker with wooden spoon to shred. Reduce heat to LOW. Stir in cilantro and cook 10 minutes. Serve with sour cream.

Makes 4 servings

White Bean Chili

  1 pound ground chicken
  3 cups coarsely chopped celery
  1 can (16 ounces) whole tomatoes, undrained and coarsely
      chopped
  1 can (15½ ounces) Great Northern beans, drained and rinsed
1½ cups coarsely chopped onions
  1 cup chicken broth
  4 teaspoons chili powder
  3 cloves garlic, minced
1½ teaspoons ground cumin
  ¾ teaspoon ground allspice
  ¾ teaspoon ground cinnamon
  ½ teaspoon pepper

Spray large nonstick skillet with cooking spray; heat over high heat until hot. Add chicken; cook until browned, breaking into pieces with fork. Add remaining ingredients to slow cooker; stir well. Cover and cook on LOW 5½ to 6 hours or until chicken is no longer pink and celery is tender.

Makes 6 servings

Chunky Vegetable Chili

2 cans (about 15 ounces *each*) Great Northern beans, rinsed and
  drained
1 cup frozen corn
1 medium onion, chopped
2 ribs celery, diced
1 can (6 ounces) tomato paste
1 can (4 ounces) diced mild green chilies, undrained
1 carrot, diced
3 cloves garlic, minced
1 tablespoon chili powder
2 teaspoons dried oregano leaves
1 teaspoon salt
1 cup water
  Assorted crackers

Combine beans, corn, onion, celery, tomato paste, green chilies, carrot,
garlic, chili powder, oregano and salt in slow cooker. Stir in water.
Cover and cook on LOW 5½ to 6 hours or until vegetables are tender.
Serve with assorted crackers. *Makes 6 servings*

Chunky Vegetable Chili

Turkey Vegetable Chili Mac

¾ pound ground turkey breast
1 can (about 15 ounces) black beans, rinsed and drained
1 can (14½ ounces) Mexican-style stewed tomatoes, undrained
1 can (14½ ounces) no-salt-added diced tomatoes, undrained
1 cup frozen corn
½ cup chopped onion
2 cloves garlic, minced
1 teaspoon Mexican seasoning
½ cup uncooked elbow macaroni
⅓ cup sour cream

Spray large skillet with nonstick cooking spray. Add turkey; cook until browned. Combine cooked turkey, beans, tomatoes, corn, onion, garlic and seasoning in slow cooker. Cover and cook on LOW 4 to 5 hours.

Stir in macaroni. Cover and cook 10 minutes; stir. Cover and cook 20 to 30 minutes or until pasta is tender. Serve with sour cream.

Makes 6 servings

Turkey Vegetable Chili Mac

Chunky Chili

1 pound lean ground beef
1 medium onion, chopped
1 tablespoon chili powder
1½ teaspoons ground cumin
2 cans (16 ounces *each*) diced tomatoes, undrained
1 can (15 ounces) pinto beans, rinsed and drained
½ cup prepared salsa
    Salt and pepper
½ cup (2 ounces) shredded Cheddar cheese
3 tablespoons sour cream
4 teaspoons sliced black olives

Heat large skillet over medium heat. Add beef and onion; cook until beef is browned and onion is tender. Drain fat. Place beef mixture, chili powder, cumin, tomatoes, beans and salsa in slow cooker; stir. Cover and cook on LOW 5 to 6 hours or until flavors are blended and chili is bubbly. Season with salt and pepper to taste. Serve with cheese, sour cream and olives.   *Makes 4 (1½-cup) servings*

Serving Suggestion: Serve with tossed green salad and cornbread muffins.

Black and White Chili

1 pound chicken tenders, cut into ¾-inch pieces
1 cup coarsely chopped onion
1 can (15½ ounces) Great Northern beans, drained
1 can (15 ounces) black beans, drained
1 can (14½ ounces) Mexican-style stewed tomatoes, undrained
2 tablespoons Texas-style chili powder seasoning mix

Spray large saucepan with nonstick cooking spray; heat over medium heat until hot. Add chicken and onion; cook and stir 5 minutes or until chicken is browned.

Combine cooked chicken, onion, beans, tomatoes and chili seasoning in slow cooker. Cover and cook on LOW 4 to 4½ hours.
                    Makes 6 (1-cup) servings

Chunky Chili

Soups & Stews

Country Chicken Chowder (page 30)

Country Chicken Chowder

   2 tablespoons margarine or butter
1½ pounds chicken tenders, cut into ½-inch pieces
   2 small onions, chopped
   2 ribs celery, sliced
   2 small carrots, sliced
   2 cups frozen corn
   2 cans (10¾ ounces *each*) cream of potato soup
1½ cups chicken broth
   1 teaspoon dried dill weed
   ½ cup half-and-half

Melt margarine in large skillet. Add chicken; cook until browned. Add cooked chicken, onions, celery, carrots, corn, soup, chicken broth and dill to slow cooker. Cover and cook on LOW 3 to 4 hours or until chicken is no longer pink and vegetables are tender.

Turn off heat; stir in half-and-half. Cover and let stand 5 to 10 minutes or just until heated through. *Makes 8 servings*

Note: For a special touch, garnish soup with croutons and fresh dill.

Hearty Cassoulet

   1 tablespoon olive oil
   1 large onion, finely chopped
   4 boneless skinless chicken thighs (about 1 pound), chopped
   ¼ pound smoked turkey sausage, finely chopped
   3 cloves garlic, minced
   1 teaspoon dried thyme leaves
   ½ teaspoon ground black pepper
   4 tablespoons tomato paste
   2 tablespoons water
   3 cans (about 15 ounces *each*) Great Northern beans, rinsed and
      drained
   ½ cup dry bread crumbs
   3 tablespoons minced fresh parsley

Heat oil in large skillet over medium heat until hot. Add onion; cook and stir 5 minutes or until onion is tender. Stir in chicken, sausage, garlic, thyme and black pepper. Cook 5 minutes or until chicken and sausage are browned.

Remove skillet from heat; stir in tomato paste and water until blended. Place beans and chicken mixture in slow cooker; cover and cook on LOW 4 to 4½ hours. Just before serving, combine bread crumbs and parsley in small bowl. Sprinkle on top of cassoulet.   *Makes 6 servings*

French-Style Pork Stew

    1 tablespoon vegetable oil
    1 pork tenderloin (16 ounces), cut into ¾- to 1-inch cubes
    1 medium onion, coarsely chopped
    1 rib celery, sliced
    ½ teaspoon dried basil leaves
    ¼ teaspoon dried rosemary leaves, crushed
    ¼ teaspoon dried oregano leaves
    2 tablespoons all-purpose flour
    1 cup chicken broth
    ½ package (16 ounces) frozen mixed vegetables
        (carrots, potatoes and peas)
    1 jar (4½ ounces) sliced mushrooms, drained
    1 package (6.2 ounces) long grain and wild rice
    2 teaspoons lemon juice
    ⅛ teaspoon ground nutmeg
      Salt and pepper to taste

Heat oil in large skillet over high heat. Add pork, onion, celery, basil, rosemary and oregano. Cook until pork is browned. Place pork mixture in slow cooker. Stir flour into chicken broth; pour into slow cooker.

Stir in frozen vegetables and mushrooms. Cover and cook on LOW 4 hours or until pork is barely pink in center. Prepare rice according to package directions, discarding spice packet, if desired.

Stir lemon juice, nutmeg and salt and pepper to taste into slow cooker. Cover and cook 15 minutes. Serve stew over rice.

Makes 4 (1-cup) servings

Beer and Cheese Soup

2 to 3 slices pumpernickel or rye bread
¼ cup finely chopped onion
2 cloves garlic, minced
¾ teaspoon dried thyme leaves
1 can (about 14 ounces) chicken broth
1 cup beer
6 ounces American cheese, shredded or diced
4 to 6 ounces sharp Cheddar cheese, shredded
½ teaspoon paprika
1 cup milk

Preheat oven to 425°F. Slice bread into ½-inch cubes; place on baking sheet. Bake 10 to 12 minutes, stirring once, or until crisp; set aside.

Combine onion, garlic, thyme, chicken broth and beer in slow cooker. Cover and cook on LOW 4 hours. Turn to HIGH. Stir cheeses, paprika and milk into slow cooker. Cook 45 to 60 minutes or until soup is hot and cheeses are melted. Stir soup well to blend cheeses. Ladle soup into bowls; top with pumpernickel croutons.   *Makes 4 (1-cup) servings*

Italian Sausage and Vegetable Stew

1 pound hot or mild Italian sausage, cut into 1-inch pieces
1 package (16 ounces) frozen mixed vegetables (onions and
green, red and yellow bell peppers)
1 can (14½ ounces) diced Italian-style tomatoes, undrained
2 medium zucchini, sliced
1 jar (4½ ounces) sliced mushrooms, drained
4 cloves garlic, minced
2 tablespoons Italian-style tomato paste

Heat large skillet over high heat until hot. Add sausage; cook about
5 minutes or until browned. Pour off any drippings.

Combine sausage, frozen vegetables, tomatoes, zucchini, mushrooms
and garlic in slow cooker. Cover and cook on LOW 4 to 4½ hours or
until zucchini is tender. Stir in tomato paste. Cover and cook 30
minutes or until juices have thickened.   *Makes 6 (1-cup) servings*

Serving Suggestion: Italian Sausage and Vegetable Stew is excellent
served with garlic bread.

Italian Sausage and
Vegetable Stew

Jambalaya

2 cups diced boiled ham
2 medium onions, coarsely chopped
2 stalks celery, sliced
½ green bell pepper, seeded and diced
1 can (28 ounces) whole tomatoes
¼ cup tomato paste
3 cloves garlic, minced
1 tablespoon minced parsley
½ teaspoon dried thyme leaves
2 whole cloves
2 tablespoons vegetable oil
1 cup uncooked long-grain converted rice
1 pound fresh or frozen shrimp, shelled and deveined

SLOW COOKER DIRECTIONS

Thoroughly mix all ingredients *except* shrimp in CROCK-POT® Slow Cooker. Cover and cook on Low 8 to 10 hours.

One hour before serving, turn CROCK-POT® Slow Cooker to High. Stir in uncooked shrimp. Cover and cook until shrimp are pink and tender.

Makes 4 to 6 servings

Chicken Stew with Dumplings

2 cups sliced carrots
1 cup chopped onion
1 large green bell pepper, sliced
½ cup sliced celery
2 cans (about 14 ounces *each*) chicken broth
⅔ cup all-purpose flour
1 pound boneless skinless chicken breasts, cut into 1-inch pieces
1 large potato, unpeeled and cut into 1-inch pieces
6 ounces mushrooms, halved
¾ cup frozen peas
1 teaspoon dried basil
¾ teaspoon dried rosemary
¼ teaspoon dried tarragon
¾ to 1 teaspoon salt
¼ teaspoon black pepper
¼ cup heavy cream

HERB DUMPLINGS

1 cup biscuit mix
¼ teaspoon dried basil
¼ teaspoon dried rosemary
⅛ teaspoon dried tarragon
⅓ cup reduced-fat (2%) milk

For stew, combine carrots, onion, bell pepper and celery in slow cooker. Stir in chicken broth, reserving 1 cup broth. Cover and cook on LOW 2 hours.

Stir flour into remaining 1 cup broth until smooth. Stir into slow cooker. Add chicken, potato, mushrooms, peas, basil, rosemary and tarragon to slow cooker. Cover and cook 4 hours or until vegetables are tender and chicken is no longer pink. Stir in salt, black pepper and heavy cream.

For biscuits, combine biscuit mix and herbs in small bowl. Stir in milk to form soft dough. Spoon dumpling mixture on top of stew in 4 large spoonfuls. Cook, uncovered, 30 minutes. Cover and cook 30 to 45 minutes or until dumplings are firm and toothpick inserted in center comes out clean. Serve in shallow bowls.   *Makes 4 servings*

Chicken Stew with Dumpling

Chinese Chicken Stew

1 pound boneless skinless chicken thighs, cut into 1-inch pieces
1 teaspoon Chinese five-spice powder
½ to ¾ teaspoon red pepper flakes
1 tablespoon peanut or vegetable oil
1 large onion, coarsely chopped
1 package (8 ounces) fresh mushrooms, sliced
2 cloves garlic, minced
1 can (about 14 ounces) chicken broth, divided
1 tablespoon cornstarch
1 large red bell pepper, cut into ¾-inch pieces
2 tablespoons soy sauce
1 tablespoon sesame oil
2 large green onions, cut into ½-inch pieces
3 cups hot cooked white rice (optional)
¼ cup coarsely chopped cilantro (optional)

Toss chicken with five-spice powder in small bowl. Season with red pepper flakes. Heat peanut oil in large skillet. Add onion and chicken; cook and stir about 5 minutes or until chicken is browned. Add mushrooms and garlic; cook and stir until chicken is no longer pink.

Combine ¼ cup broth and cornstarch in small bowl; set aside. Place cooked chicken mixture, remaining broth, bell pepper and soy sauce in slow cooker. Cover and cook on LOW 3½ hours or until peppers are tender.

Stir in cornstarch mixture, sesame oil and green onions; cook 30 to 45 minutes or until juices have thickened. Ladle into soup bowls; scoop ½ cup rice into each bowl, if desired. Sprinkle with cilantro, if desired.

Makes 6 servings (about 5 cups)

Chinese Chicken Stew

Classic French Onion Soup

¼ cup butter
3 large yellow onions, sliced
1 cup dry white wine
3 cans (about 14 ounces *each*) beef or chicken broth
½ teaspoon dried thyme
½ teaspoon salt
1 teaspoon Worcestershire sauce
1 loaf French bread, sliced and toasted
4 ounces shredded Swiss cheese
Fresh thyme for garnish

Melt butter in large skillet over high heat. Add onions; cook and stir 15 minutes or until onions are soft and lightly browned. Stir in wine.

Combine onion mixture, beef broth, thyme, salt and Worcestershire in slow cooker. Cover and cook on LOW 4 to 4½ hours. Ladle soup into 4 individual bowls; top with bread slice and cheese. Garnish with fresh thyme, if desired.   *Makes 4 servings*

Classic French Onion Soup

Smoked Sausage Gumbo

1 cup chicken broth
1 can (14½ ounces) diced tomatoes, undrained
¼ cup all-purpose flour
2 tablespoons olive oil
¾ pound Polish sausage, cut into ½-inch pieces
1 medium onion, diced
1 green bell pepper, diced
2 ribs celery, chopped
1 carrot, peeled and chopped
2 teaspoons dried oregano
2 teaspoons dried thyme
⅛ teaspoon ground red pepper
1 cup uncooked long-grain white rice

Combine broth and tomatoes in slow cooker. Sprinkle flour evenly over bottom of small skillet. Cook over high heat without stirring 3 to 4 minutes or until flour begins to brown. Reduce heat to medium; stir flour about 4 minutes. Stir in oil until smooth. Carefully whisk flour mixture into slow cooker.

Add sausage, onion, bell pepper, celery, carrot, oregano, thyme and ground red pepper to slow cooker. Stir well. Cover and cook on LOW 4½ to 5 hours or until juices are thickened.

About 30 minutes before gumbo is ready to serve, prepare rice. Cook rice in 2 cups boiling water in medium saucepan. Serve gumbo over rice.

Makes 4 servings

Note: For a special touch, sprinkle chopped parsley over each serving.

Smoked Sausage Gumbo

Beef Bourguignon

1 boneless beef sirloin steak, ½ inch thick, trimmed, cut into
    ½-inch pieces (about 3 pounds)
½ cup all-purpose flour
4 slices bacon, diced
2 medium carrots, diced
8 small new red potatoes, cut into quarters
8 to 10 mushrooms, sliced
20 to 24 fresh pearl onions
3 cloves garlic, minced
1 bay leaf
1 teaspoon dried marjoram leaves, crushed
½ teaspoon dried thyme leaves, crushed
½ teaspoon salt
    Black pepper to taste
2½ cups Burgundy wine or beef broth

Coat beef with flour, shaking off excess. Set aside.

Cook bacon in large skillet over medium heat until partially cooked. Add beef; cook until browned. Remove beef and bacon with slotted spoon.

Layer carrots, potatoes, mushrooms, onions, garlic, bay leaf, marjoram, thyme, salt, pepper, beef and bacon mixture and wine in slow cooker. Cover and cook on LOW 8 to 9 hours or until beef is tender. Discard bay leaf before serving.   *Makes 10 to 12 servings*

Beef Bourguignon

Pipin' Hot Poultry

Chicken Fajita with Cowpoke Barbecue Sauce (page 50)

Chicken Fajitas with Cowpoke Barbecue Sauce

COWPOKE BARBECUE SAUCE
- ¾ cup chopped green onions
- 3 cloves garlic, minced
- 1 can (14½ ounces) crushed tomatoes
- ½ cup ketchup
- ¼ cup water
- ¼ cup orange juice
- 2 tablespoons cider vinegar
- 2 teaspoons chili sauce
- Dash Worcestershire sauce

CHICKEN FAJITAS
- 10 ounces boneless skinless chicken breasts, cut lengthwise into 1×½-inch pieces
- 2 green or red bell peppers, thinly sliced
- 1 cup sliced onion
- 2 cups tomato wedges
- 4 (6-inch) warm flour tortillas

Combine all Cowpoke Barbecue Sauce ingredients in slow cooker. Cover and cook on HIGH 1½ hours.

Spray large nonstick skillet with nonstick cooking spray. Add chicken and cook over medium heat until browned. Reduce slow cooker heat to LOW. Add cooked chicken, bell peppers and onion to slow cooker. Stir until well coated. Cover and cook 3 to 4 hours or until chicken is no longer pink and vegetables are tender.

Add tomatoes; cover and cook 30 to 45 minutes or until heated through. Serve with warm tortillas. *Makes 4 servings*

Lemony Roasted Chicken

- 1 fryer or roasting chicken (3 to 4 pounds)
- ½ cup chopped onion
- 2 tablespoons butter
- Juice of one lemon
- 1 tablespoon fresh parsley
- 2 teaspoons grated lemon peel
- ¼ teaspoon salt
- ¼ teaspoon dried thyme leaves

Rinse chicken and pat dry with paper towels. Remove and discard any excess fat. Place onion in chicken cavity and rub skin with butter. Place chicken in slow cooker. Squeeze juice of lemon over chicken. Sprinkle with parsley, grated lemon peel, salt and thyme. Cover and cook on LOW 6 to 8 hours.

Makes 6 servings

Harvest Drums

1 package (about 1¼ pounds) PERDUE® Fresh Skinless Chicken
 Drumsticks
½ teaspoon dried Italian herb seasoning
 Salt and black pepper
3 bacon slices, diced
2 cans (14½ ounces each) pasta-ready tomatoes with cheeses
1 small onion, chopped
1 garlic clove, minced
¼ cup red wine
1 small zucchini, scrubbed and julienned
1 package (12 ounces) angel hair pasta, cooked and drained

Sprinkle chicken with Italian seasoning and salt and pepper to taste. In large, nonstick skillet over medium-low heat, cook bacon about 5 minutes, until crisp. Remove from skillet; drain and crumble. Increase heat to medium-high. Add chicken to bacon drippings (or replace drippings with 1½ tablespoons olive oil); cook 4 to 5 minutes on all sides or until brown, turning often.

In large slow cooker, combine tomatoes, bacon, onion, garlic and wine. Add chicken; cook on high 1½ to 1¾ hours, or until fork-tender. Add zucchini during last 5 minutes of cooking. Serve chicken and vegetables over angel hair pasta.

Makes 3 to 4 servings

Chicken Curry

1 small onion, sliced
2 boneless skinless chicken breast halves, cut into ¾-inch pieces
1 clove garlic, minced
1 teaspoon curry powder
¼ teaspoon ground ginger
3 tablespoons raisins
1 cup coarsely chopped apple, divided
1½ teaspoons chicken bouillon granules
1½ teaspoons all-purpose flour
⅓ cup water
¼ cup sour cream
½ teaspoon cornstarch
½ cup uncooked white rice

Combine onion, chicken, garlic, curry powder, ginger, raisins and ¾ cup chopped apple in slow cooker. Combine chicken bouillon granules, flour and water in small bowl; stir until dissolved. Add to slow cooker. Cover and cook on LOW 3½ to 4 hours or until onions are tender and chicken is no longer pink.

Combine sour cream and cornstarch in large bowl. Turn off slow cooker; remove insert to heatproof surface. Drain all cooking liquid from chicken mixture and stir into sour cream mixture. Add back to insert; stir well. Place insert back in slow cooker. Cover and let stand 5 to 10 minutes or until sauce is heated through.

Meanwhile, cook rice according to package directions. Serve chicken curry over rice; garnish with remaining ¼ cup apple.

Makes 2 servings

Note: For a special touch, sprinkle chicken with with green onion slivers just before serving.

Chicken Curry

Fusilli Pizzaiola with Turkey Meatballs

2 cans (14½ ounces *each*) no-salt-added tomatoes, undrained
1 can (8 ounces) no-salt-added tomato sauce
¼ cup chopped onion
¼ cup grated carrot
2 tablespoons no-salt-added tomato paste
2 tablespoons chopped fresh basil
1 clove garlic, minced
½ teaspoon dried thyme leaves
¼ teaspoon sugar
¼ teaspoon black pepper, divided
1 bay leaf
1 pound ground turkey breast
1 egg, lightly beaten
1 tablespoon fat-free (skim) milk
¼ cup Italian-seasoned dry bread crumbs
2 tablespoons chopped fresh parsley
8 ounces uncooked fusilli or other spiral-shaped pasta

Combine tomatoes, tomato sauce, onion, carrot, tomato paste, basil, garlic, thyme, sugar, ⅛ teaspoon black pepper and bay leaf in slow cooker. Break up tomatoes gently with wooden spoon. Cover and cook on LOW 4½ to 5 hours.

About 45 minutes before end of cooking, prepare meatballs. Preheat oven to 350°F. Combine turkey, egg and milk; blend in bread crumbs, parsley and remaining ⅛ teaspoon black pepper. With wet hands, shape mixture into small balls. Spray baking sheet with nonstick cooking spray. Arrange meatballs on baking sheet. Bake 25 minutes or until no longer pink in center.

Add meatballs to slow cooker. Cover and cook 45 minutes to 1 hour or until meatballs are heated through. Discard bay leaf. Prepare pasta according to package directions. Drain. Place in serving bowl; top with meatballs and sauce.

Makes 4 servings

*Fusilli Pizzaiola with
Turkey Meatballs*

90's-Style Slow Cooker Coq Au Vin

2 packages BUTTERBALL® Boneless Skinless Chicken Breast Fillets
1 pound fresh mushrooms, sliced thick
1 jar (15 ounces) pearl onions, drained
½ cup dry white wine
1 teaspoon thyme leaves
1 bay leaf
1 cup chicken broth
⅓ cup flour
½ cup chopped fresh parsley
   Wild rice pilaf (optional)

SLOW COOKER DIRECTIONS
Place chicken, mushrooms, onions, wine, thyme and bay leaf into slow cooker. Combine chicken broth and flour; pour into slow cooker. Cover and cook 5 hours on low setting. Add parsley. Serve over wild rice pilaf, if desired. *Makes 8 servings*

Preparation Time: 30 minutes plus cooking time

He-Man Stew

1 package (about 3½ pounds) PERDUE® Fresh Skinless Pick of the Chicken
   Salt and ground pepper
2 tablespoons olive oil
1 can (12 ounces) lite beer
1 can (28 ounces) whole plum tomatoes, drained and chopped
1 onion, sliced into rings
¼ cup spicy brown mustard
4 cups cooked elbow macaroni

Season chicken with salt and pepper to taste. In large nonstick skillet over medium-high heat, heat oil. Add chicken; cook 5 to 6 minutes on each side for larger pieces, 3 to 4 minutes on each side for smaller pieces, or until brown, turning often. In large slow cooker, combine beer, tomatoes, onion and mustard. Add chicken. Cook on high 1½ to 2 hours, or until chicken is fork-tender. Serve over macaroni.

Makes 3 to 4 servings

Turkey Tacos

1 pound ground turkey
1 medium onion, chopped
1 can (6 ounces) tomato paste
½ cup chunky salsa
1 tablespoon chopped cilantro
½ teaspoon salt
8 taco shells
1 tablespoon butter
1 tablespoon all-purpose flour
¼ teaspoon salt
⅓ cup milk
½ cup sour cream
Ground red pepper

Brown turkey and onion in large skillet over medium heat. Combine turkey mixture, tomato paste, salsa, cilantro and salt in slow cooker. Cover and cook on LOW 4 to 5 hours. Spoon ¼ cup turkey mixture into each taco shell; keep warm.

Melt butter in small saucepan over low heat. Stir in flour and salt. Carefully stir in milk. Cook over low heat until thickened. Remove from heat. Combine sour cream and sprinkle of ground red pepper in small bowl. Stir into hot milk mixture. Return to heat; cook over low heat 1 minute, stirring constantly. Spoon over taco filling.   *Makes 8 tacos*

Meatball Grinders

¼ cup chopped onion
1 can (15 ounces) diced tomatoes, drained and juice reserved
1 can (8 ounces) reduced-sodium tomato sauce
2 tablespoons tomato paste
1 teaspoon dried Italian seasoning
1 pound ground chicken
½ cup fresh whole-wheat or white bread crumbs (1 slice bread)
1 egg white, lightly beaten
3 tablespoons finely chopped fresh parsley
2 cloves garlic, minced
¼ teaspoon salt
⅛ teaspoon black pepper
4 small hard rolls, split
2 tablespoons grated Parmesan cheese

Combine onion, diced tomatoes, ½ cup reserved juice, tomato sauce, tomato paste and Italian seasoning in slow cooker. Cover and cook on LOW 3 to 4 hours or until onions are soft.

During the last 30 minutes of cooking time, prepare meatballs. Combine chicken, bread crumbs, egg white, parsley, garlic, salt and pepper in medium bowl. With wet hands form mixture into 12 to 16 meatballs. Spray medium nonstick skillet with cooking spray; heat over medium heat until hot. Add meatballs; cook about 8 to 10 minutes or until well browned on all sides. Remove meatballs to slow cooker; cook 1 to 2 hours or until meatballs are no longer pink in centers and are heated through.

Place 3 to 4 meatballs in each roll. Divide sauce evenly; spoon over meatballs. Sprinkle with cheese.   *Makes 4 servings*

Meatball Grinder

Greek-Style Chicken Stew

  2 cups cubed peeled eggplant
  2 cups sliced mushrooms
  ¾ cup coarsely chopped onion
  2 cloves garlic, minced
  1 teaspoon dried oregano leaves
  ½ teaspoon dried basil leaves
  ½ teaspoon dried thyme leaves
1¼ cups low-sodium chicken broth
1½ teaspoons all-purpose flour
  6 skinless chicken breasts (about 2 pounds)
    Additional all-purpose flour
  3 tablespoons dry sherry or low-sodium chicken broth
  ¼ teaspoon salt
  ¼ teaspoon black pepper
  1 can (14 ounces) artichoke hearts, drained
12 ounces uncooked wide egg noodles

Combine eggplant, mushrooms, onion, garlic, oregano, basil, thyme, broth and flour in slow cooker. Cover and cook on HIGH 1 hour.

Coat chicken very lightly with flour. Generously spray large nonstick skillet with cooking spray; heat over medium heat until hot. Cook chicken 10 to 15 minutes or until browned on all sides.

Remove vegetables to bowl with slotted spoon. Layer chicken in slow cooker; return vegetables to slow cooker. Add sherry, salt and pepper. Reduce heat to LOW and cover and cook 6 to 6½ hours or until chicken is no longer pink in center and vegetables are tender.

Stir in artichokes; cover and cook 45 minutes to 1 hour or until heated through. Cook noodles according to package directions. Serve chicken stew over noodles. *Makes 6 servings*

Greek-Style Chicken Stew

Beef, Pork & Lamb

Broccoli and Beef Pasta (page 64)

Broccoli and Beef Pasta

2 cups broccoli florets *or* **1 package (10 ounces) frozen broccoli, thawed**
1 medium onion, thinly sliced
½ teaspoon dried basil leaves
½ teaspoon dried oregano leaves
½ teaspoon dried thyme leaves
1 can (14½ ounces) Italian-style diced tomatoes, undrained
¾ cup beef broth
1 pound lean ground beef
2 cloves garlic, minced
2 tablespoons tomato paste
2 cups cooked rotini pasta
3 ounces shredded Cheddar cheese or grated Parmesan cheese

Layer broccoli, onion, basil, oregano, thyme, tomatoes and beef broth in slow cooker. Cover and cook on LOW 2½ hours.

Combine beef and garlic in large nonstick skillet; cook over high heat 6 to 8 minutes or until meat is no longer pink, breaking meat apart with wooden spoon. Pour off drippings. Add beef mixture to slow cooker. Cover and cook 2 hours.

Stir in tomato paste. Add pasta and cheese. Cover and cook 30 minutes or until cheese melts and mixture is heated through.

Makes 4 servings

Glazed Corned Beef

1½ cups water
1 medium onion, sliced
3 strips fresh orange peel
2 whole cloves
3 to 4 pounds corned beef (round or rump cut)
  Additional whole cloves (optional)
  Glaze (recipe follows)

Combine water, onion, orange peel and cloves in slow cooker. Add corned beef, fat side up, to slow cooker. Cover and cook on LOW 7 to 9 hours or until fork-tender.

Remove corned beef from slow cooker. Score top of corned beef; insert additional cloves to decorate, if desired.

About 30 minutes before serving, place corned beef in ovenproof pan. Preheat oven to 375°F. Prepare Glaze; spoon over corned beef. Bake 20 to 30 minutes, basting occasionally with Glaze.

Makes 8 to 10 servings

Glaze

3 tablespoons honey
2 tablespoons frozen orange juice concentrate, thawed
2 teaspoons prepared mustard

Combine honey, orange juice concentrate and mustard in large bowl.

Barbecued Beef

   3 pounds boneless chuck roast
1½ cups ketchup
   ¼ cup packed brown sugar
   ¼ cup red wine vinegar
   2 tablespoons Dijon-style mustard
   2 tablespoons Worcestershire sauce
   1 teaspoon liquid smoke flavoring
   ½ teaspoon salt
   ¼ teaspoon black pepper
   ¼ teaspoon garlic powder
      Sandwich buns

SLOW COOKER DIRECTIONS
Place chuck roast in CROCK-POT® Slow Cooker. Combine remaining ingredients in large bowl. Pour barbecue sauce mixture over chuck roast. Cover and cook on Low 8 to 10 hours or 4 to 5 hours on High. Remove chuck roast from CROCK-POT® Slow Cooker; shred meat with fork. Place shredded meat back in CROCK-POT® Slow Cooker. Stir meat to evenly coat with sauce. Spoon meat onto sandwich buns and top with additional barbecue sauce, if desired.   *Makes 12 servings*

Barbecued Beef

Vegetable-Stuffed Pork Chops

4 double pork loin chops, well trimmed
Salt and black pepper
1 can (15¼ ounces) corn, drained
1 small onion, chopped
1 green bell pepper, seeded and chopped
1 cup Italian-style seasoned dry bread crumbs
½ cup uncooked, long-grain converted rice
1 can (8 ounces) tomato sauce
Fresh salad (optional)

Cut pocket in each pork chop, cutting from edge nearest bone. Lightly season pockets with salt and pepper to taste. Combine corn, onion, bell pepper, bread crumbs and rice in large bowl. Stuff pork chops with vegetable-rice mixture. Secure along fat side with wooden toothpicks.

Pour any remaining vegetable-rice mixture into slow cooker. Add stuffed pork chops to slow cooker. Moisten top of each pork chop with tomato sauce. Pour any remaining tomato sauce over top. Cover and cook on LOW 8 to 10 hours or until done.

Remove pork chops to serving platter. Serve with vegetable-rice mixture and fresh salad, if desired. *Makes 4 servings*

Beefy Tostada Pies

2 teaspoons olive oil
1½ cups chopped onions
2 pounds ground beef
1 teaspoon chili powder
1 teaspoon ground cumin
1 teaspoon salt
2 cloves garlic, minced
1 can (15 ounces) tomato sauce
1 cup sliced black olives
8 flour tortillas
4 cups shredded Cheddar cheese
Sour cream, salsa and chopped green onion (optional)

Heat oil in large skillet over medium heat. Add onions and cook until tender. Add ground beef, chili powder, cumin, salt and garlic; cook until browned. Stir in tomato sauce; heat through. Stir in black olives.

Make foil handles using three 18×2-inch strips of heavy foil. Crisscross foil to form spoke design. Place in slow cooker. Lay one tortilla on foil strips. Spread with meat sauce and layer of cheese. Top with another tortilla, meat sauce and cheese. Repeat layers ending with cheese. Cover and cook on HIGH 1½ hours. To serve, lift out of slow cooker using foil handles and transfer to serving platter. Discard foil. Cut into wedges. Serve with sour cream, salsa and chopped green onion, if desired.   *Makes 4 to 5 servings*

Suzie's Sloppy Joes

      3 pounds lean ground beef
      1 cup chopped onion
      3 cloves garlic, minced
    1¼ cups ketchup
      1 cup chopped red bell pepper
      5 tablespoons Worcestershire sauce
      4 tablespoons brown sugar
      3 tablespoons prepared mustard
      3 tablespoons vinegar
      2 teaspoons chili powder
        Hamburger buns

Brown ground beef, onion, and garlic in small saucepan. Drain fat.

Combine ketchup, bell pepper, Worcestershire sauce, brown sugar, mustard, vinegar and chili powder in slow cooker. Stir in beef mixture. Cover and cook on LOW 6 to 8 hours. Spoon into hamburger buns.

Makes 8 to 10 servings

Lamb in Dill Sauce

2 large boiling potatoes, peeled and cut into 1-inch cubes
½ cup chopped onion
1½ teaspoons salt
½ teaspoon black pepper
½ teaspoon dried dill weed *or* 4 sprigs fresh dill
1 bay leaf
2 pounds lean lamb stew meat, cut into 1-inch cubes
1 cup plus 3 tablespoons water, divided
2 tablespoons all-purpose flour
1 teaspoon sugar
2 tablespoons lemon juice
Fresh dill (optional)

Layer potatoes, onion, salt, pepper, dill, bay leaf, lamb and 1 cup water in slow cooker. Cover and cook on LOW 6 to 8 hours.

Remove lamb and potatoes with slotted spoon; cover and keep warm. Remove and discard bay leaf. Turn heat to HIGH. Stir flour and remaining 3 tablespoons water in small bowl until smooth. Add half of cooking juices and sugar. Mix well and return to slow cooker. Cover and cook 15 minutes. Stir in lemon juice. Return lamb and potatoes to slow cooker. Cover and cook 10 minutes or until heated through. Garnish with fresh dill, if desired. *Makes 6 servings*

Give Me a Side of...

Arroz con Queso (page 74)

Arroz con Queso

1 can (16 ounces) whole tomatoes, mashed
1 can (16 ounces) Mexican-style beans
1½ cups uncooked long-grain converted rice
1 large onion, finely chopped
1 cup cottage cheese
1 can (4 ounces) green chili peppers, drained, seeded and chopped
2 tablespoons vegetable oil
3 cloves garlic, minced
2 cups grated Monterey Jack or processed cheese, divided

SLOW COOKER DIRECTIONS

Lightly grease CROCK-POT® Slow Cooker. Mix all ingredients *except* 1 cup grated cheese in large bowl. Pour mixture into CROCK-POT® Slow Cooker. Cover and cook on Low 6 to 9 hours.

Just before serving, sprinkle with reserved grated cheese.

Makes 6 to 8 servings

Mrs. Grady's Beans

½ pound lean ground beef
1 small onion, chopped
8 bacon strips, chopped
1 can (about 15 ounces) pinto beans, undrained
1 can (about 15 ounces) butter beans, rinsed and drained, reserving ¼ cup liquid
1 can (about 15 ounces) kidney beans, rinsed and drained
¼ cup ketchup
2 tablespoons molasses
½ teaspoon dry mustard
½ cup granulated sugar
¼ cup packed brown sugar

Brown ground beef, onion and bacon in medium saucepan over high heat. Stir in beans and liquid; set aside.

Combine ketchup, molasses and mustard in medium bowl. Mix in sugars. Stir ketchup mixture into beef mixture; mix well. Transfer to slow cooker. Cover and cook on LOW 2 to 3 hours or until heated through.   *Makes 6 to 8 servings*

Sunshine Squash

   1 butternut squash (about 2 pounds) peeled, seeded and diced
   1 can (14½ ounces) tomatoes, undrained
   1 can (about 15 ounces) corn, drained
   1 medium onion, coarsely chopped
   1 clove garlic, minced
   1 green bell pepper, seeded and cut into 1-inch pieces
   1 canned green chili, coarsely chopped
   ½ cup chicken broth
   ½ teaspoon salt
   ¼ teaspoon black pepper
   1 tablespoon plus 1½ teaspoons tomato paste

Combine all ingredients *except* tomato paste in slow cooker. Cover and cook on LOW 6 hours or until squash is tender.

Remove about ¼ cup cooking liquid and blend with tomato paste. Stir into slow cooker. Cook 30 minutes or until mixture is slightly thickened and heated through.   *Makes 6 to 8 servings*

Louise's Broccoli Casserole

    2 packages (10 ounces each) frozen broccoli spears, thawed and
        cut up
    1 can (10¾ ounces) condensed cream of celery soup
 1¼ cups grated sharp Cheddar cheese, divided
    ¼ cup minced green onions
    1 cup crushed saltine crackers or potato chips

SLOW COOKER DIRECTIONS

Grease CROCK-POT® Slow Cooker. In large bowl, combine broccoli,
celery soup, 1 cup cheese and onions. Pour into CROCK-POT® Slow
Cooker. Sprinkle top with crushed crackers, then with remaining cheese.
Cover and cook on Low 5 to 6 hours or on High 2½ to 3 hours.

Makes 4 to 6 servings

Note: If desired, casserole may be spooned into a baking dish and
garnished with additional grated cheese and broken potato chips; bake
5 to 10 minutes in 400°F oven.

Louise's Broccoli Casserole

Bean and Cornbread Casserole

    1 medium onion, chopped
    1 medium green bell pepper, chopped
    2 cloves garlic, minced *or* ¼ teaspoon garlic powder
    1 can (16 ounces) red kidney beans, undrained
    1 can (16 ounces) pinto beans, undrained
    1 can (16 ounces) no-salt-added diced tomatoes, undrained
    1 can (8 ounces) no-salt-added tomato sauce
    1 teaspoon chili powder
    ½ teaspoon black pepper
    ½ teaspoon prepared mustard
    ⅛ teaspoon hot sauce
    1 cup yellow cornmeal
    1 cup all-purpose flour
 2½ teaspoons baking powder
    1 tablespoon sugar
    ½ teaspoon salt
 1¼ cups milk
    ½ cup egg substitute
    3 tablespoons vegetable oil
    1 can (8½ ounces) no-salt-added cream-style corn

SLOW COOKER DIRECTIONS

Lightly grease CROCK-POT® Slow Cooker. In skillet over medium heat, cook onion, bell pepper and garlic until tender. Transfer to CROCK-POT® Slow Cooker. Stir in kidney beans and pinto beans. Add diced tomatoes and juice, tomato sauce, seasonings, mustard and hot sauce. Cover and cook on High for 1 hour.

In large bowl, combine cornmeal, flour, baking powder, sugar and salt. Stir in milk, egg substitute, vegetable oil and corn. Spoon evenly over bean mixture. There may be leftover cornbread depending on size of CROCK-POT® Slow Cooker being used (if there's remaining cornbread, spoon into greased muffin tins and bake at 375°F 30 minutes or until golden brown). Cover and cook on High 1½ to 2 more hours. Serve.

Makes 6 to 8 servings

New England Baked Beans

4 slices uncooked bacon, chopped
3 cans (15 ounces *each*) Great Northern beans, rinsed and
    drained
¾ cup water
1 small onion, chopped
2 cloves garlic, minced
3 tablespoons firmly packed brown sugar
3 tablespoons maple syrup
3 tablespoons unsulphured molasses
½ teaspoon salt
½ teaspoon dry mustard
⅛ teaspoon black pepper
½ bay leaf
⅓ cup canned diced tomatoes, well drained

Cook bacon in large skillet until almost cooked but not crispy. Drain on paper towels.

Combine bacon and all remaining ingredients in slow cooker. Cover and cook on LOW 6 to 8 hours or until onions are tender and mixture is thickened. Remove bay leaf before serving.　　*Makes 4 to 6 servings*

New England Baked Beans

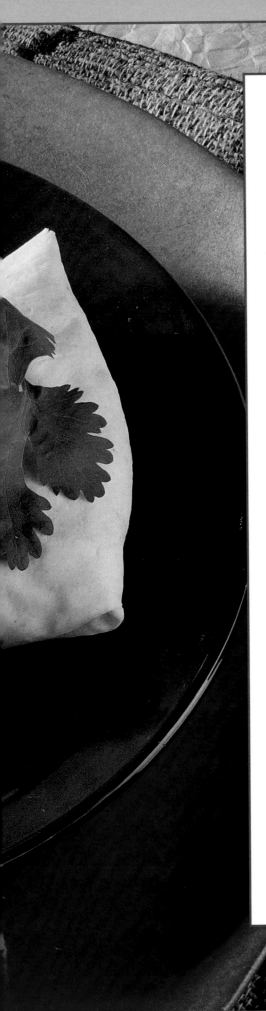

Totally Vegetarian

Bean and Vegetable Burrito (page 84)

Bean and Vegetable Burritos

2 tablespoons chili powder
2 teaspoons dried oregano leaves
1½ teaspoons ground cumin
1 large sweet potato, peeled and diced
1 can black beans or pinto beans, rinsed and drained
4 cloves garlic, minced
1 medium onion, halved and thinly sliced
1 jalapeño pepper, seeded and minced
1 green bell pepper, chopped
1 cup frozen corn, thawed and drained
3 tablespoons lime juice
1 tablespoon chopped cilantro
¾ cup (3 ounces) shredded Monterey Jack cheese
4 (10-inch) flour tortillas
Sour cream (optional)

* Jalapeño peppers can sting and irritate the skin; wear rubber gloves when handling peppers and do not touch eyes. Wash hands after handling.

Combine chili powder, oregano and cumin in small bowl. Set aside.

Layer sweet potato, beans, half of chili powder mix, garlic, onion, jalapeño pepper, bell pepper, remaining half of chili powder mix and corn in slow cooker. Cover and cook on LOW 5 hours or until sweet potato is tender. Stir in lime juice and cilantro.

Preheat oven to 350°F. Spoon 2 tablespoons cheese in center of each tortilla. Top with 1 cup filling. Fold all 4 sides to enclose filling. Place burritos seam side down on baking sheet. Cover with foil and bake 20 to 30 minutes or until heated through. Serve with sour cream, if desired.

Makes 4 servings

Meatless Sloppy Joes

2 cups thinly sliced onions
2 cups chopped green bell peppers
1 can (about 15 ounces) kidney beans, drained and mashed
1 can (8 ounces) tomato sauce
2 cloves garlic, finely chopped
2 tablespoons ketchup
1 tablespoon mustard
1 teaspoon chili powder
Cider vinegar (optional)
4 sandwich rolls, halved

Combine all ingredients *except* rolls in slow cooker. Cover and cook on LOW 5 to 5½ hours or until vegetables are tender. Serve on rolls.

Makes 4 servings

Pesto Rice and Beans

1 can (15 ounces) Great Northern beans, rinsed and drained
1 can (14 ounces) vegetable broth
¾ cup uncooked long-grain white rice
1½ cups frozen cut green beans, thawed and drained
½ cup prepared pesto sauce
Additional grated Parmesan cheese (optional)

Combine Great Northern beans, vegetable broth and rice in slow cooker. Cover and cook on LOW 2 hours.

Stir in green beans; cover and cook 1 hour or until rice and beans are tender. Turn off slow cooker and remove insert to heatproof surface. Stir in pesto sauce and additional Parmesan cheese, if desired. Let stand, covered, 5 minutes or until cheese has melted. Serve immediately.

Makes 8 servings

Savory Bean Stew

1 cup frozen vegetable seasoning blend (onions, celery, red and green bell peppers)
1 can (15½ ounces) chick-peas, rinsed and drained
1 can (15 ounces) pinto beans, rinsed and drained
1 can (15 ounces) black beans, rinsed and drained
1 can (14½ ounces) diced tomatoes with roasted garlic, undrained
¾ teaspoon dried thyme leaves
¾ teaspoon dried sage leaves
½ to ¾ teaspoon dried oregano leaves
1 tablespoon all-purpose flour
¾ cup vegetable broth, divided

POLENTA
¾ cup yellow cornmeal
¾ teaspoon salt

Combine frozen vegetable blend, chick-peas, beans, tomatoes and herbs in slow cooker. Stir flour into ½ cup vegetable broth; pour into bean mixture and stir well. Cover and cook 4 hours or until vegetables are tender and juice is thickened.

Meanwhile, prepare polenta. Bring 3 cups water to a boil in large saucepan. Reduce heat; gradually stir in cornmeal and salt. Cook 5 to 8 minutes or until cornmeal thickens. Keep warm.

Stir remaining ¼ cup broth into slow cooker. Spread polenta on plate and top with stew.   *Makes 6 (1-cup) servings*

Savory Bean Stew

Eggplant Italiano

1¼ pounds eggplant, cut into 1-inch cubes
2 medium onions, thinly sliced
2 ribs celery, cut into 1-inch pieces
1 tablespoon olive oil, divided
1 can (16 ounces) diced tomatoes, undrained
3 tablespoons tomato sauce
½ cup pitted ripe olives, cut in half
2 tablespoons balsamic vinegar
1 tablespoon sugar
1 tablespoon capers, drained
1 teaspoon dried oregano or basil leaves, crushed
  Salt and black pepper to taste
  Fresh basil leaves, leaf lettuce and red jalapeño pepper for
    garnish

Combine eggplant, onions, celery, oil, tomatoes and tomato sauce in slow cooker. Cover and cook on LOW 3½ to 4 hours or until eggplant is tender.

Stir in olives, vinegar, sugar, capers and oregano. Season with salt and pepper. Cover and cook 45 minutes to 1 hour or until heated through. Garnish, if desired.

Makes 6 servings

Savory Bean Stew with Cheddar-Cornmeal Dumplings

1 can (28 ounces) tomatoes, undrained and chopped
2 cups chopped red bell peppers
1 can (15 ounces) black beans, rinsed and drained
1 can (15 ounces) pinto beans, rinsed and drained
2 small zucchini, coarsely chopped
2 large onions, chopped
1 poblano chili, seeded and chopped
½ cup sliced celery
3 cloves garlic, minced
3 tablespoons chili powder
2 teaspoons ground cumin
1 teaspoon dried oregano leaves
½ teaspoon salt, divided
½ cup all-purpose flour
½ cup cornmeal
1 teaspoon baking powder
½ teaspoon sugar
2 tablespoons cold butter or margarine
¼ cup shredded Cheddar cheese
1 tablespoon minced fresh cilantro
½ cup milk

Combine tomatoes, red bell peppers, beans, zucchini, onions, poblano chili, celery, garlic, chili powder, cumin, oregano, and ¼ teaspoon salt in slow cooker. Cover and cook on HIGH 4 to 4½ hours or until vegetables are tender.

During the last hour of cooking, prepare dumplings. Combine flour, cornmeal, baking powder, sugar and remaining ¼ teaspoon salt in medium bowl. Cut in butter with pastry blender or two knives until mixture resembles coarse crumbs.

Stir in cheese and cilantro. Pour milk into flour mixture; blend with wooden spoon just until dry ingredients are moistened. Drop dumpling dough into 6 mounds on top of stew. Cover and cook 40 minutes to 1 hour or until toothpick inserted into dumplings comes out clean.

Makes 6 servings

*Savory Bean Stew with
Cheddar-Cornmeal Dumplings*

Sweet Potato Casserole

2 cans (18 ounces *each*) sweet potatoes, drained and mashed
⅓ cup margarine or butter, melted
2 tablespoons granulated sugar
2 tablespoons plus ⅓ cup brown sugar, divided
1 tablespoon orange juice
2 eggs, beaten
½ cup milk
⅓ cup chopped pecans
2 tablespoons all-purpose flour
2 tablespoons margarine or butter, melted

SLOW COOKER DIRECTIONS

Lightly grease CROCK-POT® Slow Cooker. Mix sweet potatoes, ⅓ cup margarine, granulated sugar and 2 tablespoons brown sugar in large bowl. Beat in orange juice, eggs and milk. Transfer to CROCK-POT® Slow Cooker.

Combine pecans, ⅓ cup brown sugar, flour and 2 tablespoons margarine. Spread over sweet potatoes. Cover and cook on High 3 to 4 hours. Serve. *Makes 6 to 8 servings*

Index